JACKIE ROBINSON

THE BEATLES

NATIONAL GEOGRAPHIC KiDS

LITTLE KIDS
FIRST
BIG
BOOK OF
WHO

Jill Esbaum

CONTENTS

Leonardo da Vinci
Thomas Edison
George Washington
  Carver
John Muir
Albert Einstein
Jane Goodall
Rachel Carson
Galileo Galilei

MICHELANGELO'S "PIETÀ"

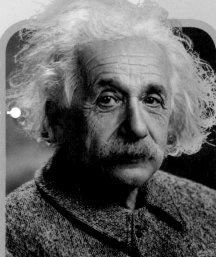

INTRODUCTION

This book introduces curious young readers to some of the most interesting and important people in history. Each profile answers questions about someone whose life has had great impact on the rest of us, from artists and inventors to scientists and human rights leaders. Also included are mini-profiles of men and women from all over the world. You may have heard of some of these people before. Others may be new to you.

NATIONAL GEOGRAPHIC'S *LITTLE KIDS FIRST BIG BOOK OF WHO* IS ORGANIZED IN CHRONOLOGICAL ORDER AND PRESENTS A RANGE OF MEN AND WOMEN WITH DIFFERENT INTERESTS AND TALENTS:

ARTISTS

From the talented Michelangelo to the musical sensation that was the Beatles, readers are introduced to artists of all kinds: painters, sculptors, writers, and musicians.

INVENTORS AND SCIENTISTS

Marie Curie was the first woman to win a Nobel Prize, and Galileo Galilei built one of the world's first telescopes. These individuals are at the forefront of our world's progress. Their profiles demonstrate just how far we have come.

EXPLORERS

They travel the world, reach new heights, and discover the unimaginable. Readers will learn just what it takes to be an adventurous, record-breaking voyager through reading about these explorers who have made history.

HUMAN RIGHTS LEADERS

Leaders such as Malala Yousafzai and Martin Luther King, Jr., highlight both the importance and the danger associated with standing up for what is right. These brave men and women illustrate how and why we have the rights that we have today.

HOW TO USE THIS BOOK

Colorful **PHOTOGRAPHS** illustrate each spread, supporting the text.

POP-UP FACTS and quotes sprinkled throughout provide added information about each man or woman.

At **29,029 FEET** (8,848 m) high, Mount Everest is the **TALLEST MOUNTAIN** on Earth.

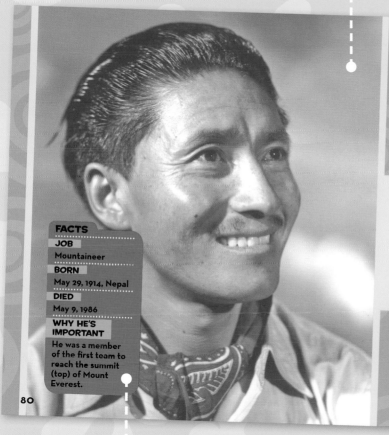

FACTS

JOB
Mountaineer

BORN
May 29, 1914, Nepal

DIED
May 9, 1986

WHY HE'S IMPORTANT
He was a member of the first team to reach the summit (top) of Mount Everest.

80

TENZING NORGAY

Many dangers face those who want to climb to the top of Mount Everest. The air is thin at high altitudes, so it is hard for human lungs to get enough oxygen. Storms can move in quickly and bring high winds and very cold temperatures. Climbers often fall. Some might step into a deep gash in the ice called a crevasse. Dangerous avalanches can strike at any time. They sweep away everything and everybody in their path.

81

FACT BOXES give the young reader a quick look at a person's basic background and what they're most known for.

MORE FOR PARENTS

In the back of the book you will find parent tips, including fun activities that relate to individuals in the book, along with a helpful glossary.

An **ARCHAEOLOGIST** is someone who **LEARNS** how **HUMANS LIVED** in the past by studying things found in cities, homes, and burial sites.

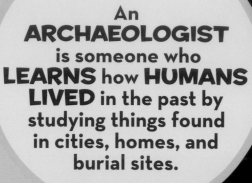

FACTS

JOB

King of Egypt

BORN

1341 B.C., Egypt

DIED

1323 B.C.

WHY HE'S IMPORTANT

The 1922 discovery of the tomb where Tut was buried helped historians learn about ancient Egypt.

KING TUT

When a king died in ancient Egypt, his oldest son was named the next king. It didn't matter how old the son was at the time.

King Tutankhamun— King Tut, for short—was only nine years old when he became Egypt's king in 1332 B.C. Historians didn't know much about Tutankhamun until 1922. This was the year a British archaeologist named Howard Carter uncovered Tut's tomb in the Valley of the Kings.

HOWARD CARTER HELPS OPEN TUT'S TOMB, EGYPT, IN 1922.

Tut was only 19 when he died. He was buried with golden figures and jewelry, oils and perfumes, even favorite toys from his childhood. Scenes showing Tut's funeral and his journey to the afterlife were painted on the walls.

BURIAL CHAMBER OF KING TUTANKHAMUN

Mediterranean Sea

EGYPT

Nile River

Red Sea

Valley of the Kings ★

Map Key
— Present-day country boundary

Howard Carter searched the tomb carefully for two years and he found another room. Inside that room was a coffin. It was opened to reveal a smaller coffin. That coffin was opened to reveal a third coffin that was made of gold. Inside the golden coffin was Tut's mummified body, untouched for more than 3,000 years.

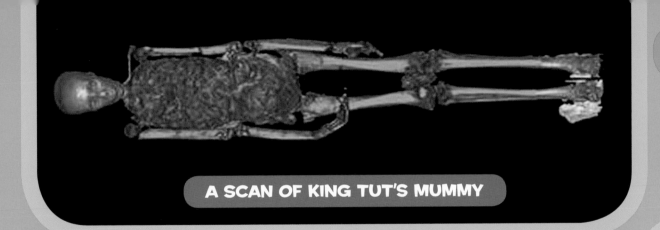

A SCAN OF KING TUT'S MUMMY

It took Howard **CARTER** and other workers **17 YEARS** to find everything in King Tut's four-room **TOMB.**

ILLUSTRATION OF THE LAYERS OF KING TUT'S BURIAL SHRINES AND COFFINS

Scientists studied Tut's remains and learned that he had broken his leg shortly before he died. They think he probably got an infection that led to his death.

Tut was Egypt's king for about ten years before he died. While he was king he was likely told what to do by older people. He remains one of the most famous Egyptian kings in history because his tomb has given us so much information about his life.

ARISTOTLE

A **PHILOSOPHER** is a person who studies ideas about **LIFE, KNOWLEDGE,** the nature of the **UNIVERSE,** and right and wrong.

Aristotle was 17 years old when he left his hometown in northern Greece. He went to study in the city of Athens at the school of a famous teacher named Plato. The young man loved learning so much that he stayed and taught at Plato's school for 20 years.

Aristotle wanted to know why people acted the way they did, how they solved their problems, and how they got along with others.

FACTS

JOB
Philosopher, teacher, writer

BORN
About 384 B.C., Greece

DIED
About 322 B.C.

WHY HE'S IMPORTANT
He was a great thinker. His ideas about how people should learn and behave and understand life still shape the way we live and think today.

He was interested in other things, too. He wanted to know about land and ocean animals, about weather and stars and planets. He was interested in theater and religion and politics and music and poetry.

After Plato died, Aristotle took a job in the Greek kingdom of Macedon. There he taught 13-year-old Alexander. Alexander would become king when he was only 20 years old.

"Wishing to be **FRIENDS** is **QUICK** work, but **FRIENDSHIP** is a slow ripening **FRUIT.**"

"**GOOD HABITS** formed at **YOUTH** make all the **DIFFERENCE.**"

FROM A PAINTING OF ARISTOTLE BY G. MOCETTO

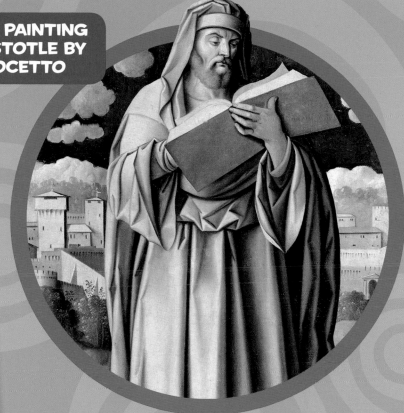

ONE OF ARISTOTLE'S WRITINGS

Aristotle later went back to Athens and opened his own school. He called it the Lyceum. He spent most of the rest of his life there—teaching, studying, and writing. Some of his writings still exist and are read today.

15

The
RENAISSANCE
(about A.D. 1400–1600)
was a time in history when
people were learning
a lot about **ART,**
LITERATURE, and
MUSIC.

FACTS

JOB

Artist, engineer

BORN

March 6, 1475,
Italy

DIED

February 18, 1564

WHY HE'S
IMPORTANT

He was one of
the most talented
artists of all time.

THE STATUE "DAVID"

MICHELANGELO

Michelangelo was a sculptor, painter, architect, and poet who lived during the Italian Renaissance period.

Michelangelo first worked as a sculptor. Two of his most famous sculptures are the "Pietà" and the statue "David." No artist before him had created such life-like sculptures. Soon he became famous for his amazing work.

THE "PIETÀ"

One day Pope Julius II approached the young sculptor to ask an important question. Would he please consider painting the ceiling of the Sistine Chapel?

At first, Michelangelo didn't want to do the work. He didn't consider himself a painter. It was also a very big job and would take years to complete. Still, he decided to try.

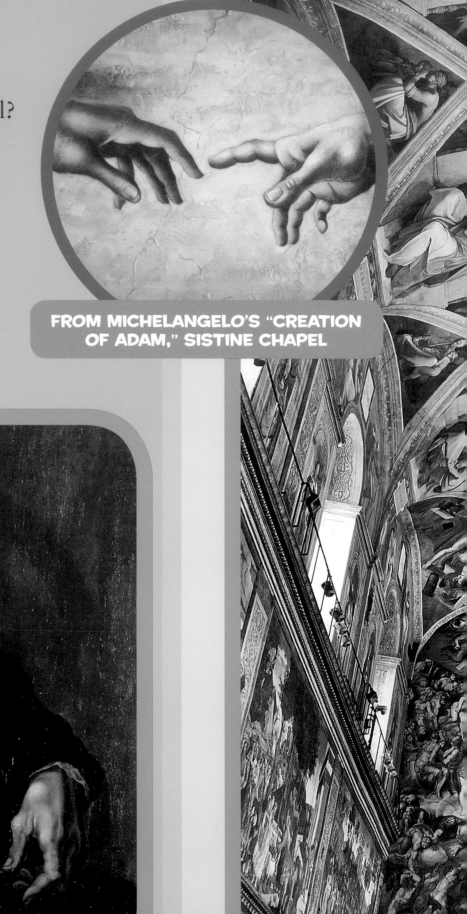

FROM MICHELANGELO'S "CREATION OF ADAM," SISTINE CHAPEL

"PORTRAIT OF MICHELANGELO," BY JACOPINO DEL CONTE

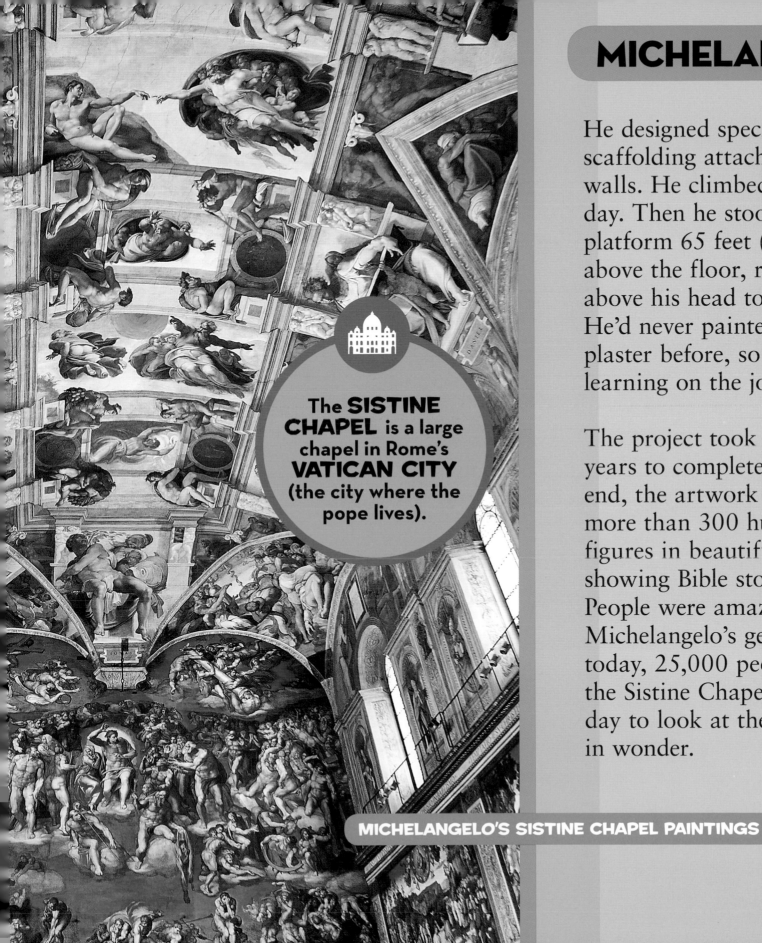

MICHELANGELO

The **SISTINE CHAPEL** is a large chapel in Rome's **VATICAN CITY** (the city where the pope lives).

He designed special scaffolding attached to the walls. He climbed it every day. Then he stood on a platform 65 feet (20 m) above the floor, reaching above his head to paint. He'd never painted on plaster before, so he was learning on the job.

The project took four long years to complete. In the end, the artwork contained more than 300 human figures in beautiful scenes showing Bible stories. People were amazed by Michelangelo's genius. Even today, 25,000 people visit the Sistine Chapel every day to look at the ceiling in wonder.

MICHELANGELO'S SISTINE CHAPEL PAINTINGS

WILLIAM SHAKESPEARE

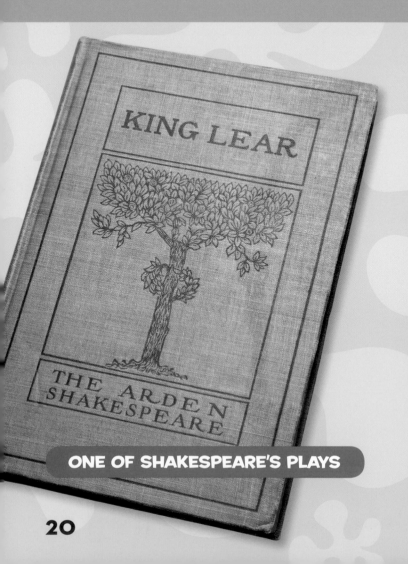

ONE OF SHAKESPEARE'S PLAYS

William Shakespeare is the most famous playwright the world has ever known.

Shakespeare started out as an actor. He performed in London with a group called the King's Men. He also wrote poetry and plays. When some of his poetry and plays were published, he made enough money to buy a large house for his family. The house was in a town called Stratford-upon-Avon, where he had grown up. Stratford was a four-day journey from London, where Shakespeare worked. Since it was so far, he may have visited his family only once a year!

FACTS

JOB
Playwright, poet

BORN
April 23, 1564,
England

DIED
Early April 1616

WHY HE'S IMPORTANT
The plays and poetry he wrote hundreds of years ago are still performed and enjoyed today.

A **PLAYWRIGHT** is a person who **WRITES PLAYS** for actors to perform live on a **STAGE.**

21

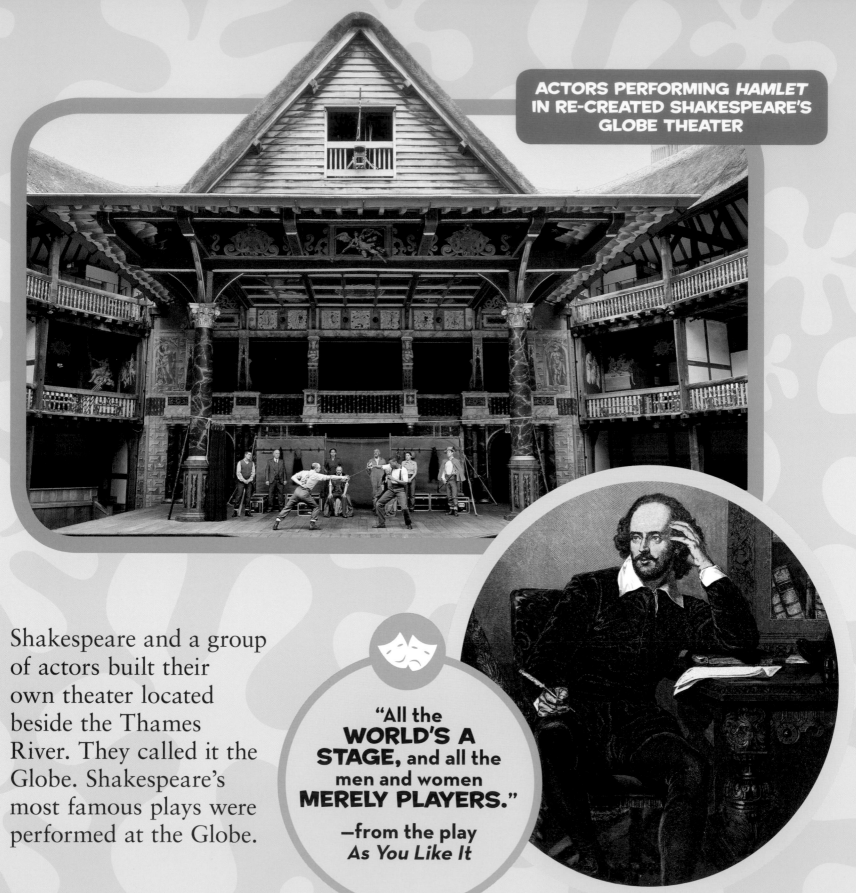

ACTORS PERFORMING *HAMLET* IN RE-CREATED SHAKESPEARE'S GLOBE THEATER

Shakespeare and a group of actors built their own theater located beside the Thames River. They called it the Globe. Shakespeare's most famous plays were performed at the Globe.

"All the **WORLD'S A STAGE**, and all the men and women **MERELY PLAYERS.**"

—from the play *As You Like It*

Some of his plays are sad and gloomy. Others are very funny. He also created plays about the lives of the kings of England. In some plays, characters fall in love. In others, characters make bad decisions or have a hard time getting along with others.

"This **ABOVE ALL:** to thine **OWN SELF** be **TRUE.**"
—from the play *Hamlet*

ACTORS PERFORMING *THE TAMING OF THE SHREW*

The Tragicall Historie of
HAMLET
Prince of Denmarke.

Enter two Centinels. {now call'd Bernardo & Francisco —

1. STand: who is that?
2. 'T is I.
2. O you come most carefully vpon your watch,
And if you meete *Marcellus* and *Horatio*,
The partners of my watch, bid them make haste.
1. I will: See who goes there.
        Enter *Horatio* and *Marcellus*.
Hor. Friends to this ground.
        And leegemen to the Dane,
        who hath releeued you?

William Shakespeare was a genius at coming up with stories and characters that felt real to audiences of his time—and still do today.

23

FACTS

JOB
Novelist

BORN
December 16, 1775, England

DIED
July 18, 1817

WHY SHE'S IMPORTANT
She was one of England's greatest writers. She helped invent the novel as a type of literature, and she made women and girls the main characters in her books.

"One man's **WAYS** may be **AS GOOD** as another's, but we all like **OUR OWN** best."

—from the book *Persuasion*

JANE AUSTEN

Austen grew up in a middle-class family. The Austen children were educated mostly at home, thanks to their father's large library. For fun, they played games or read aloud to each other. Austen loved funny, romantic stories.

Jane and her brothers and sister often wrote plays to perform for the rest of the family.

ONE OF AUSTEN'S MOST FAMOUS BOOKS, *PRIDE AND PREJUDICE*

She wrote her first stories for herself and her family to enjoy. When their father died in 1805, Jane, her sister, Cassandra, and their mother did not have much money. They lived with relatives, including some of Jane's brothers, who were already grown up.

In 1809 Jane's brother Henry bought a home for his mother and sisters. The ladies moved in and Jane began writing novels for publication (to be sold to others). She was hoping to earn some money for her family. Since well-raised ladies weren't supposed to write novels, Jane didn't put her own name on her books.

"There is no **CHARM** equal to **TENDERNESS** of **HEART.**"

AUSTEN'S HOME AT CHAWTON, HAMPSHIRE

She used the pseudonym "a Lady." She asked Henry to send her writings to a publisher.

Her novels sold well and many are still popular today. Jane was able to live a quiet life, because only her family knew she was the writer of her books. It wasn't until after she died that Henry told the world who the writer really was.

AUSTEN'S WRITING TABLE AT CHAWTON

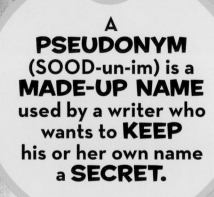

A **PSEUDONYM** (SOOD-un-im) is a **MADE-UP NAME** used by a writer who wants to **KEEP** his or her own name a **SECRET.**

27

SEQUOYAH

Sequoyah was also known as George Gist. He could speak many languages and was often used as an interpreter between his Cherokee tribe and the white people moving into their area.

An **INTERPRETER** is a person who helps others **COMMUNICATE** by **TRANSLATING** one language into another.

Ohio River

Mississippi River

KENTUCKY

Cherokee lands

TENNESSEE

VIRGINIA

NORTH CAROLINA

SOUTH CAROLINA

ALABAMA

GEORGIA

ATLANTIC OCEAN

Map Key
— Present-day state boundary

FACTS

JOB

Silversmith

BORN

About 1776, U.S.A.

DIED

1843

WHY HE'S IMPORTANT

A member of the Cherokee tribe, he created the first Native American writing system.

The **CHEROKEE** lived in an area that now includes the states of **ALABAMA, GEORGIA, KENTUCKY, NORTH CAROLINA, SOUTH CAROLINA, TENNESSEE,** and **VIRGINIA.**

Sequoyah saw how the white settlers could communicate with one another not just by speaking but also by reading marks on paper.

He also noticed that many Cherokees were learning to speak English. Sequoyah worried about that. He wondered what would happen if young Cherokees stopped speaking their own language. Would the Cherokee language be forgotten?

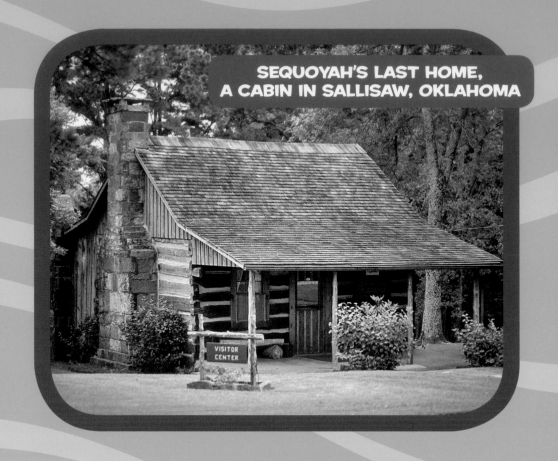

SEQUOYAH'S LAST HOME, A CABIN IN SALLISAW, OKLAHOMA

Cherokee Alphabet

Sequoyah's **SYLLABARY** can be learned today at Tennessee's **SEQUOYAH** Birthplace **MUSEUM.**

The Cherokee language had no alphabet to use to make words. Sequoyah decided to change that. He built a cabin in the woods to do his work. For 12 years he experimented with pictures and shapes and symbols. Finally, he was ready to share his syllabary (SIL-uh-BARE-ee). He had 85 characters that each stood for a Cherokee sound, or syllable. Putting them together would make words.

Other Cherokees were excited to learn Sequoyah's written symbols. In 1827, tribal leaders used it to write the tribe's own constitution (rules for living). A year later, the Cherokee people began publishing their own newspaper with articles printed in both English and Cherokee. The syllabary also gave them a way to write down Cherokee tradition, so they would never be forgotten.

THE *CHEROKEE PHOENIX*, PRINTED IN BOTH ENGLISH AND SEQUOYAH'S CHEROKEE SCRIPT

31

The Voyage of **DISCOVERY** took two years and covered more than **8,000 MILES** (12,875 km).

SACAGAWEA

FACTS

JOB

Interpreter, guide

BORN

About 1788, U.S.A.

DIED

1812

WHY SHE'S IMPORTANT

She was the only woman on Lewis and Clark's Voyage of Discovery. She served as an interpreter on the journey.

Sacagawea was a Native American born into the Shoshone tribe in what is now the state of Idaho. She was about 12 years old when she was kidnapped by an enemy tribe called the Hidatsa. A few years later, they sold her to a French-Canadian trader named Toussaint Charbonneau. He made her one of his wives.

IDAHO'S SALMON RIVER

33

In 1803, America bought a large area of land from France in what was called the Louisiana Purchase. President Thomas Jefferson hired his personal secretary, Meriwether Lewis, to explore the area. Lewis and his co-commander, William Clark, left the city of St. Louis on May 14, 1804. They had about 40 other men with them. They called this journey the Voyage of Discovery.

WILLIAM CLARK

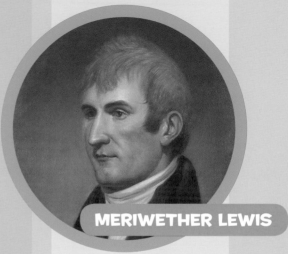

MERIWETHER LEWIS

BRITISH TERRITORY

OREGON COUNTRY

UNITED STATES

Route of Lewis & Clark

SPANISH TERRITORY

Louisiana Purchase

Map Key
— 1804 boundary

ROUTE TAKEN BY LEWIS AND CLARK

The group traveled by boat and on foot. They reached what is now North Dakota on October 26, 1804. The group settled in to spend the winter there. This is where they met Sacagawea and eventually hired her to be an interpreter on their journey. By springtime, the group was off to discover more of the West.

Sacagawea was a better choice than anybody could have imagined. She helped the group communicate with the Native Americans they met. When Native Americans saw her and her baby son with the group, they knew this was not a war party. No warriors would travel with a woman and a baby.

After the expedition, Sacagawea and her family returned to the Hidatsa tribe, where it is believed she became sick and died at about age 24. When her son was 10 years old, his father took him to St. Louis. There he was adopted by William Clark and his wife. They raised him as their own and made sure he received an education.

ONE GROUP of Native Americans the group met was led by a man whom Sacagawea **RECOGNIZED AS THE BROTHER** she hadn't seen since she was kidnapped years before. She was excited to see him. **SHE CRIED HAPPY TEARS.**

In **2000,** the United States **HONORED** Sacagawea by using her **IMAGE** on one-dollar **GOLD COINS.**

ABRAHAM LINCOLN

Abraham Lincoln was born in a one-room log cabin in Kentucky, U.S.A. When he was seven years old, the family moved to the Indiana Territory. Lincoln did not go to school very often. Instead he worked to help support his family. When he wasn't working, Lincoln was reading. He borrowed books from anybody he could.

LINCOLN'S BIRTHPLACE, HODGENVILLE, KENTUCKY

TERRITORY:
When Lincoln was a child, more and more **PEOPLE** were **MOVING** into the American **WEST**. Many of these **LANDS** were called territories. They later became **STATES.**

FACTS

JOB
Lawyer, United States president

BORN
February 12, 1809, U.S.A.

DIED
April 15, 1865

WHY HE'S IMPORTANT
He was the president who brought the United States together after the Civil War and ended slavery.

When Lincoln was 21 years old, his family moved to a town in Illinois. The next year, Lincoln moved to a different town in Illinois. Before long, everybody knew this tall man who told funny stories with a country accent. He was chosen to represent his area in the state capital. He also taught himself law and became a lawyer. Later he was elected to the U.S. House of Representatives. In 1860 he became the 16th President of the United States.

PAINTING OF THE LINCOLN FAMILY

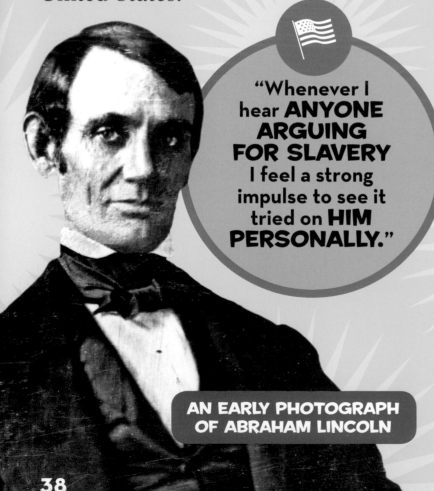

"Whenever I hear **ANYONE ARGUING FOR SLAVERY** I feel a strong impulse to see it tried on **HIM PERSONALLY.**"

AN EARLY PHOTOGRAPH OF ABRAHAM LINCOLN

At this time slavery existed across the southern states. Lincoln's belief that slavery was wrong made people in the southern states angry. They decided to start their own country called the Confederate States of America. Both the North and South were willing to fight for their beliefs. The Civil War began soon after.

The Civil War started on April 12, 1861, and lasted for four years. During the war, on January 1, 1863, Lincoln announced that slaves were free. This was called the Emancipation Proclamation.

In 1864 Lincoln was reelected. Union forces (soldiers from northern states) won the war. It ended on April 9, 1865. Southern states rejoined the North. A few days later, President Lincoln and his wife, Mary, went to see a play. A man named John Wilkes Booth was angry at Lincoln over the war. Booth shot Lincoln at the theater. Lincoln died the next day.

Today Abraham Lincoln is remembered as one of the greatest U.S. presidents. His actions helped reunite the North and South after the war. He ended slavery. Most of all, he believed in the idea stated in the Declaration of Independence that ALL people are created equal and deserve freedom.

The **13TH AMENDMENT** to the U.S. Constitution made **SLAVERY ILLEGAL** in the United States. It was **PASSED** a few months **AFTER** Lincoln **DIED.**

THE LINCOLN MEMORIAL, WASHINGTON, D.C.

FACTS

JOB

Doctor

BORN

February 3, 1821, England

DIED

May 31, 1910

WHY SHE'S IMPORTANT

She was the first female doctor in the United States. She inspired other women to follow their dreams.

Many **WOMEN** unofficially **"DOCTORED"** others, but a medical **SCHOOL** education was **OFF-LIMITS** to them.

Any time young Elizabeth Blackwell felt sick, she was treated by a male doctor. That's because there were no female doctors in England. When Elizabeth was 11 years old, her family moved to the United States. There were no female doctors there either.

Back then, most people believed that women couldn't be doctors. They believed that women were too delicate to see bloody wounds and too sensitive to perform surgery. Also, most men were horrified by the idea of a woman examining their bodies.

1974 U.S. POSTAGE STAMP HONORING ELIZABETH BLACKWELL

ELIZABETH BLACKWELL

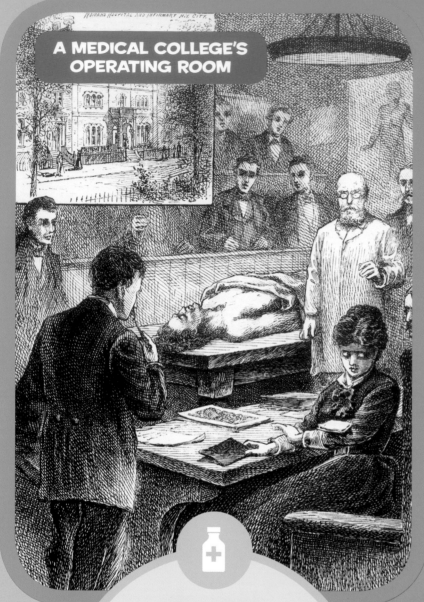

A MEDICAL COLLEGE'S OPERATING ROOM

Blackwell didn't think it made sense that women weren't allowed to become doctors. Weren't there plenty of women who would make wise and caring doctors?

Blackwell taught school through her teen years and beyond. In her spare time she studied every medical book she could get her hands on. At last, when she was 26, Blackwell had learned all she could from books. She needed to go to medical school to finish her education.

"It is **NOT EASY** to be a **PIONEER**—but oh, it is fascinating! I would **NOT TRADE** one moment, even the worst **MOMENT**, for all the **RICHES** in the world."

BLACKWELL FAMILY (ELIZABETH STANDING ON LEFT)

School after school turned her down. Geneva Medical School in New York thought her request was so crazy that they made a joke of it. They asked their all-male students to vote: Should they let her in or not? The students voted YES. They were joking too, and wanted to see what would happen next. The school let Elizabeth Blackwell enroll. They didn't think she would last long.

ELIZABETH Blackwell graduated with the **HIGHEST GRADES** in her **CLASS.**

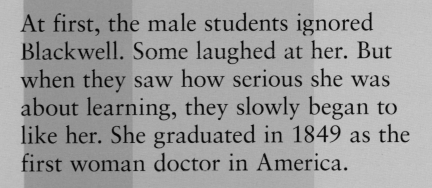

At first, the male students ignored Blackwell. Some laughed at her. But when they saw how serious she was about learning, they slowly began to like her. She graduated in 1849 as the first woman doctor in America.

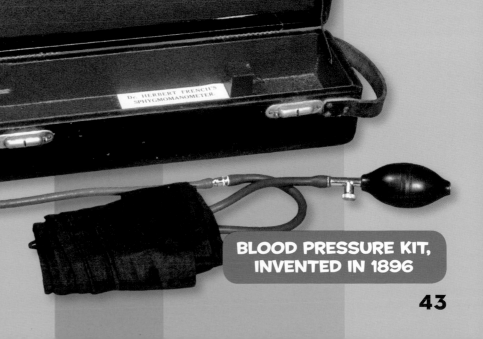

BLOOD PRESSURE KIT, INVENTED IN 1896

MEET MORE INVENTORS & SCIENTISTS

1847–1931, U.S.A. As a young child, Thomas Edison's parents pulled him out of school. Why? His teacher told them he was too active and his big head proved something was wrong with his brain. Edison was, in fact, very smart. He grew up and invented a way to bring electricity to cities and homes. He improved the lightbulb, the battery, and more. Edison was able to use his brain to invent many wonderful things.

THOMAS EDISON

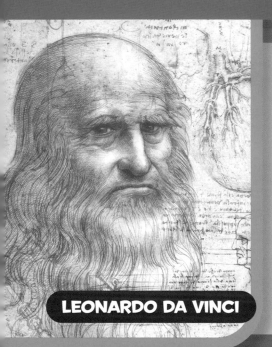

1452–1519, **Italy.** Leonardo da Vinci was one of the most well-known people of the Renaissance period. He's the artist who painted the "Mona Lisa" and "The Last Supper." Leonardo filled notebooks with ideas for inventions such as water wheels, flying machines, parachutes, and diving suits. He was also a scientist, a mathematician, and an engineer. He is still famous today.

LEONARDO DA VINCI

GEORGE WASHINGTON CARVER

1864–1943, U.S.A. George Washington Carver was the first African American to graduate from Iowa State University, where he studied plants. After college, he became a teacher. He also experimented with new ways to use the peanut. Carver found ways to turn peanuts into dye, ink, soap, glue, and even gasoline.

JOHN MUIR

1838–1914, **Scotland.** John Muir always loved nature. He loved visiting the Sierra Nevada mountains and Yosemite Valley. He spent his life fighting to protect these and other wilderness areas. In 1892 Muir founded the Sierra Club. Today this organization continues his work to protect the great outdoors.

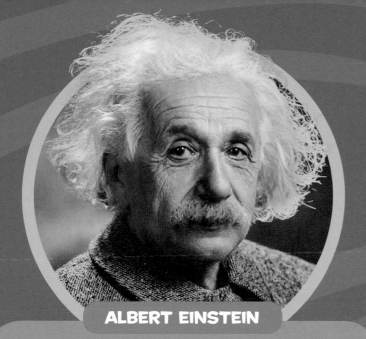

ALBERT EINSTEIN

1879–1955, Germany. Albert Einstein was a genius. He conducted experiments to learn more about many things, including electricity, heat, light, and sound. He is best known for his theory of relativity. Scientists later used the theory of relativity to invent things, such as televisions, remote controls, and lasers. Since he was so smart, his brain was studied for years after he died. It is kept at New Jersey's Princeton University Medical Center.

1934– , England. Jane Goodall lived with and studied wild chimpanzees in Africa for 40 years. She learned things about chimps that nobody else knew. She discovered that chimps communicate with each other using a language made up of about 20 sounds. She learned that they make and use tools. They also hug to comfort each other. Today she travels around the world asking people to protect natural places and allow wild animals to live in peace.

JANE GOODALL

RACHEL CARSON

1907–1964, U.S.A. In 1962, scientist Rachel Carson wrote a book called *Silent Spring*. In it, she said chemicals used to kill plant-damaging bugs also killed songbirds. Her book led to the banning of a bad chemical called DDT that had nearly wiped out all the bald eagles. Carson's book also sparked many new laws created to protect our environment.

GALILEO GALILEI

1564–1642, Italy. People used to believe that the Earth was the center of the universe. Galileo built one of the first telescopes and used it to prove that this wasn't true. The truth was that Earth and other planets moved around the sun. His experiments showed people that thinking something was true wasn't enough. They had to find ways to prove it.

ISABELLA BIRD

ROCKY MOUNTAIN NATIONAL PARK, U.S.A. (ABOVE), AND 12 APOSTLES, AUSTRALIA (BELOW)

Isabella Bird was always tired and weak as a child. When she was 22 years old, a doctor told her family that a long journey would be good for her. Bird set sail from England to visit America.

The young woman sent long letters home to her sister describing the places she saw and the things she did. Someone decided her letters would make a great book. After all, not many Englishwomen got to travel through America alone. The book was called *An Englishwoman in America* and it was very popular.

FACTS

JOB

Traveler, explorer

BORN

October 15, 1831, England

DIED

October 7, 1904

WHY SHE'S IMPORTANT

She traveled all over the world, visiting and exploring places no other Englishwoman had been. She also wrote books about her experiences.

Isabella's book *A LADY'S LIFE IN THE ROCKY MOUNTAINS* was so popular that the publisher had to reprint the book **SEVEN** times.

HAWAII'S MAUNA KEA VOLCANO (FRONT), AND MAUNA LOA VOLCANO (BACKGROUND)

Isabella Bird was the first woman asked to join **LONDON'S ROYAL GEOGRAPHIC SOCIETY,** an organization of explorers and people who **STUDIED** the **INFORMATION** brought back by **EXPLORERS.**

After her trip, Bird stayed home in England for many years. She felt sick most of the time. By 1872, both of her parents had died. There was no reason for Isabella to stay in England. She left again to visit Australia, New Zealand, and Hawaii. In Hawaii she climbed the Mauna Kea and Mauna Loa volcanoes. Each are more than 13,000 feet (3,962 m) high!

BIRD (ON HORSEBACK) READY TO EXPLORE KOREA

Next, Bird came back to America. She rode the Transcontinental Railroad through the western United States. She also took a horseback tour through the Rocky Mountains. Her guide was the tough-as-nails Rocky Mountain Jim. With him, she even climbed 14,000-foot (4,267-m)-high Long's Peak.

Isabella Bird enjoyed good health when she was outside of England. She was less than five feet (1.5 m) tall but carried heavy camera equipment on her trips to take pictures for her books. She went on to explore China, India, Japan, Korea, Kurdistan, Malaysia, Morocco, Persia (now called Iran), Singapore, Tibet, Turkey, and Vietnam.

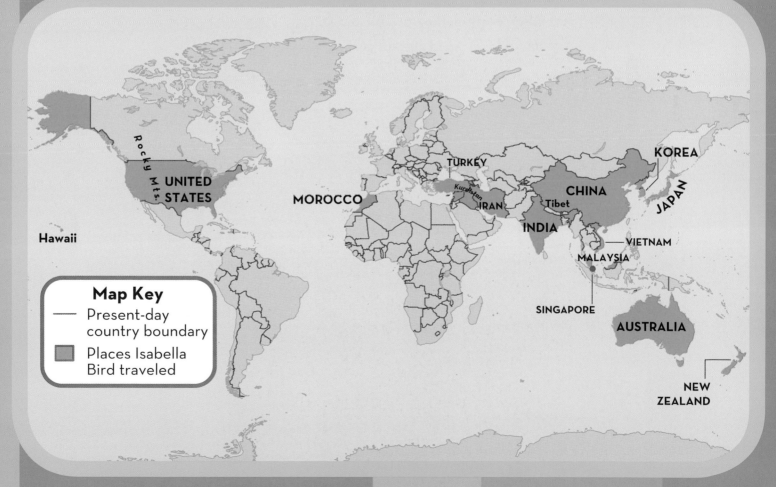

Map Key

— Present-day country boundary

▨ Places Isabella Bird traveled

JOB

Explorer

BORN

August 8, 1866, U.S.A.

DIED

March 9, 1955

WHY HE'S IMPORTANT

He was the first person to reach the North Pole.

"I felt profoundly **GRATEFUL** that I had the **HONOR** of representing my race."

MATTHEW HENSON

MATTHEW HENSON ON DECK
OF THE *ROOSEVELT*, 1906

By the late 1800s, the North Pole was one of the few places on Earth where people had never been. Teams of explorers from many countries tried and failed to reach it.

One of the most determined was an American, Admiral Robert E. Peary. Reaching the North Pole was Peary's life goal. Luckily, Peary had a secret weapon: a man named Matthew Henson.

Henson had been orphaned when he was 11 years old. He then worked as a ship's cabin boy for six years. In that time he learned to read, write, navigate by the stars, tie sailors' knots, and fix just about anything.

By late 1908, Henson had assisted Peary on seven failed tries for the North Pole. Matthew Henson was successful at something else. He had become friends with the Inuit, a group of people who lived near the North Pole. He'd learned their language, customs, and survival skills. He knew how to build and drive a dogsled, how to build an igloo, and how to hunt. Henson's friendship with the Inuit and the survival skills they taught him would help him and Peary achieve their goal of reaching the North Pole.

INUIT, also known as ESKIMOS, are people who live in northern CANADA, northern GREENLAND, and parts of ALASKA.

HENSON, WITH THREE INUITS AND A SLED DOG

HENSON IN GREENLAND, DRESSED IN ARCTIC GEAR

It was **MANY, MANY YEARS** before Henson got the **RECOGNITION** he **DESERVED.**

On April 6, 1909, Henson, Peary, four Inuit guides, and 40 dogs finally reached the North Pole. They traveled across ice for six weeks. They survived hunger and weakness, terrible snowstorms, and below freezing temperatures. Peary was 45 minutes behind Henson. He was being pulled on a sled because he had lost eight toes to frostbite on an earlier trip.

Even though Matthew Henson reached the North Pole first, he was not given credit because he was African American. At the time, African Americans didn't always get the credit they deserved. Peary was the one who received a medal from President Theodore Roosevelt. Peary also went down in the history books as the first man to the North Pole.

Today scientists aren't certain Peary and Henson reached the exact North Pole. The spot is hard to pinpoint since it is not on land but on drifting sea ice. But if they did, Matthew Henson was the one who got there first.

MARIE CURIE

Marie Sklodowska wanted to study science at the University of Warsaw in Poland. But it was an all-male school, and they wouldn't let her in. So instead, she traveled to France and studied at the University of Paris. While there, Marie met another young scientist, Pierre Curie. He would eventually become her husband. They would become two of the most famous scientists in the world.

FACTS

JOB
Scientist

BORN
November 7, 1867, Poland

DIED
July 4, 1934

WHY SHE'S IMPORTANT
She was the first woman to win a Nobel Prize. She was the only woman to win in two different fields of science: physics and chemistry. She discovered the chemical elements polonium and radium.

"One never notices **WHAT HAS BEEN DONE;** one can only see what **REMAINS TO BE DONE.**"

"I believe that **SCIENCE HAS GREAT BEAUTY.**"

Radioactivity fascinated Curie. She wanted to know all about it. Marie and Pierre worked hard to learn everything they could. Together, along with another scientist, Henri Becquerel (who had first discovered radioactivity), they won a Nobel Prize in physics in 1903 for their discoveries.

Curie worked every day with radioactive materials. She carried test tubes of radium in the pockets of her lab coat. This constantly exposed her body to high levels of radiation. Unfortunately, scientists didn't realize it was deadly until much later.

Curie loved science, research, and discovering secrets of the physical world. Her research led to better x-rays and improved cancer treatment. Her life's work and success opened doors for other women scientists.

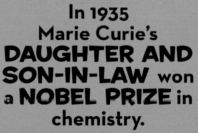

In 1935 Marie Curie's **DAUGHTER AND SON-IN-LAW** won a **NOBEL PRIZE** in chemistry.

5e Arrt

RUE PIERRE ET MARIE CURIE
1859-1906   1867-1934
PHYSICIENS, DÉCOUVREURS DE RADIUM

STREET IN FRANCE NAMED FOR PIERRE AND MARIE CURIE

Even though Gandhi's **FIRST NAME WAS MOHANDAS,** followers called him Mahatma, which means **"GREAT SOUL."**

FACTS

JOB
Lawyer, activist

BORN
October 2, 1869, India

DIED
January 30, 1948

WHY HE'S IMPORTANT
He was the leader of India's struggle for independence. He also created peaceful ways to protest unfair laws.

India was ruled by England for almost 200 years. That means India did not make the laws for its own people. Those laws came from England. Mohandas Gandhi didn't think that was right.

MOHANDAS GANDHI

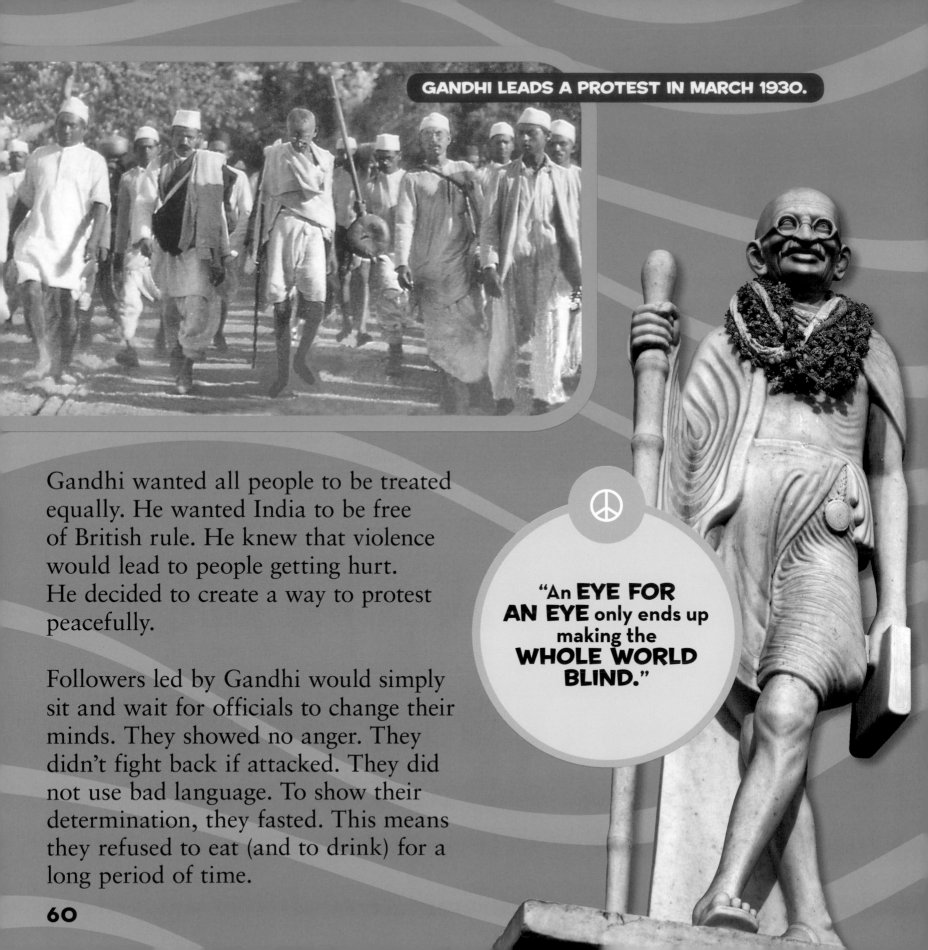

Gandhi wanted all people to be treated equally. He wanted India to be free of British rule. He knew that violence would lead to people getting hurt. He decided to create a way to protest peacefully.

Followers led by Gandhi would simply sit and wait for officials to change their minds. They showed no anger. They didn't fight back if attacked. They did not use bad language. To show their determination, they fasted. This means they refused to eat (and to drink) for a long period of time.

"An **EYE FOR AN EYE** only ends up making the **WHOLE WORLD BLIND.**"

60

With the help of Gandhi's nonviolent movement, India broke free from England. The country declared independence in 1947. Gandhi lived to see India's independence. But the following year Gandhi was assassinated by a man who didn't agree with his beliefs.

Gandhi's peaceful ways are still admired and copied by people around the world trying to bring about change. In the United States, they were very important in the civil rights movement.

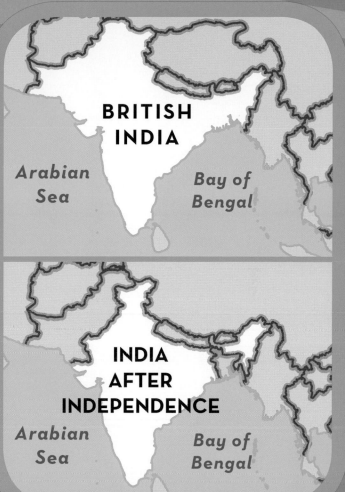

BRITISH INDIA

Arabian Sea

Bay of Bengal

INDIA AFTER INDEPENDENCE

Arabian Sea

Bay of Bengal

GANDHI SPINNING FIBER, 1925

"The **FUTURE DEPENDS** on what you do **TODAY.**"

AMELIA EARHART

When Amelia Earhart was a child, airplanes were new and exciting. She was 23 years old when a pilot at an air show offered her a ride in his small, open-cockpit plane.

Earhart wanted to look like a pilot. She cut her hair short to look like other women pilots she had seen. She also bought a leather jacket. She slept in the jacket for three nights so it wouldn't look so new and stiff.

JOB

Pilot

BORN

July 24, 1897,
U.S.A.

DIED

? (declared legally
dead in January
1939)

**WHY SHE'S
IMPORTANT**

First woman pilot
to fly solo (alone)
across the Atlantic
Ocean. She was also
the first person to
fly solo across the
Pacific Ocean.

"By the time
I had got **TWO**
or **THREE
HUNDRED FEET**
off the ground, I
knew I had to
FLY."

"After **SCARING** most of the **COWS** in the neighborhood, I pulled up in a farmer's **BACKYARD.**"

CHARLES LINDBERGH WITH HIS AIRPLANE

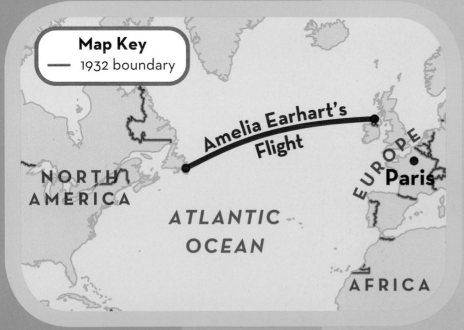

Map Key
— 1932 boundary

Amelia Earhart's Flight

NORTH AMERICA

EUROPE

Paris

ATLANTIC OCEAN

AFRICA

In 1927, Charles Lindbergh flew solo across the Atlantic Ocean. Five years later, Earhart was the first woman to do so. She hoped to land in Paris, France, as Lindbergh had done, but thick clouds, strong winds, and ice buildup on her wings forced her to land in a pasture in Ireland.

From then on, reporters and photographers followed her everywhere. People couldn't get enough of Amelia Earhart.

After her solo flight across the Atlantic Ocean, Earhart was the first woman awarded the Distinguished Flying Cross.

Earhart believed that women could do anything men could do. She set many records for speed and distance, but she wanted to do something big... really big. She wanted to fly around the world.

"I have a feeling that there is just about one more **GOOD FLIGHT** left in my system, and I hope this **TRIP** is it."

EARHART AND NOONAN WITH A MAP OF THE PACIFIC OCEAN

She decided to do it with a man named Fred Noonan as her navigator. Earhart and Noonan had flown almost all the way around the Earth when something happened. Their plane disappeared while flying through cloudy skies over the Pacific Ocean. No one ever found Earhart, Noonan, or their plane.

MEET MORE EXPLORERS

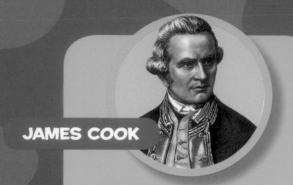

1728–1779, England. Captain James Cook was good at mapping coastlines. His government sent him to different places, including the Southern Hemisphere. While there he looked for a new continent and found the east coast of Australia. He named this land New South Wales. Cook's work provided others with maps and information to make their own discoveries.

LADY HESTER STANHOPE

1776–1839, England. In the early 1800s Lady Hester Stanhope sailed away from England looking for adventure. She went to Egypt, where she learned to speak Arabic and Turkish. Then she spent years traveling the Middle East. On her journey, she heard a rumor about buried treasure in an ancient city in Syria. She excitedly decided to organize the first archaeological dig to find it, but nothing was found.

NAIN SINGH RAWAT

1830–1895, India. Rawat was a surveyor (somebody who measures land and writes down its features for mapmakers). He was also a spy for the British. They asked Rawat to sneak into the country of Tibet to gather information about its rivers, roads, and mountains. This helped the British when they later went into Tibet to try to get control of the country.

GERTRUDE BELL

1868–1926, England. After graduating from college, Gertrude Bell traveled to Iran to visit her uncle. She enjoyed it so much that she wanted to see more of the Middle East and Asia. She made connections with many important people. This led the English to use her as a spy during World War I.

JUNKO TABEI

1939- , Japan. Junko Tabei became hooked on mountain climbing after scaling Japan's Mount Nasu with a teacher when she was just ten years old. She went on to become the first woman mountain climber to reach the summit of Mount Everest. By 1992 she had climbed the highest mountains on all seven continents. Between her climbs, she works to keep mountains clean by urging climbers to leave no garbage behind after a climb.

FERDINAND MAGELLAN

1480-1521, Portugal. Ferdinand Magellan was the first person to sail from Europe to Asia by heading west. All other people had sailed to the east. It was a brave choice because many people believed the world was flat and ships could sail off the edge. Magellan was killed by a poison arrow during the journey and didn't make it home. His ship's crew did make it back to Europe. This was important because it meant they did not fall off the edge of the Earth! It proved the Earth was round.

AMYR KLINK

1955- , Brazil. Amyr Klink pushed his small boat away from a beach in Namibia, Africa, in June 1984 to row alone across the South Atlantic Ocean. He rowed and rowed. One hundred days later he reached Brazil. He has written books about the experience and his other record-breaking solo rows and sails.

MARCO POLO

1254-1324, Italy. Marco Polo was a trader. He traveled from Italy to China and other parts of Asia. He wanted to find new markets for trading. After 24 years, he came home with many ideas new to Europeans. Polo wrote a book about his experiences that helped others understand Asia and its people.

GOLDA MEIR

Golda Meir came from a Russian Jewish family. When she was eight years old, Golda and her family moved to Milwaukee, Wisconsin, U.S.A. Even in grade school, she began to show her leadership abilities by raising money to buy textbooks for students who could not afford them. She graduated at the top of her eighth grade class. Golda's father then wanted her to start thinking about finding a husband. She wanted to go to high school.

18-YEAR-OLD GOLDA MEIR

FACTS

JOB
Prime minister

BORN
May 3, 1898, Ukraine

DIED
December 8, 1978

WHY SHE'S IMPORTANT
First woman to become prime minister of Israel. She was only the third woman in the world to be named a country's prime minister.

Meir and her husband once **LIVED** in a **KIBBUTZ** (a farm in Israel where many people live and work together). There she became an **EXPERT** on raising **CHICKENS.**

69

Golda got her way. She started high school and worked after class to help pay for her school supplies. She and her parents continued to argue about her schooling. Golda wasn't happy about that, so she moved to Colorado, U.S.A., to live with her older sister. A year later her parents wrote her to say they were sorry, and she moved back to Wisconsin to finish high school. Then she went to college to become a teacher.

MEIR ARRIVES IN LONDON, ENGLAND, IN 1958.

✡ "**TRUST YOURSELF.** Create the kind of self that you will be **HAPPY** to live with all your **LIFE.**"

While Meir was growing up, Jewish people lived in diaspora—a word that means people moving from their original homeland. Non-Jewish people treated many of them horribly, especially before and during World War II.

During **WORLD WAR II,** Adolph Hitler's **NAZI** Germany imprisoned and killed six million **JEWISH** people.

MEIR MEETS WITH U.S. PRESIDENT GERALD FORD IN 1976.

Like other Jewish people, Meir wanted Israel to be made into a place where Jews could live in peace. She moved to Palestine in 1921, hoping to help make that happen. In 1948 it did happen. The United Nations voted to set aside part of the Palestine region to create the country of Israel. Since then, living in peace has been very difficult. The Jewish and Palestinian people have had many conflicts with each other.

Golda Meir worked all of her adult life for Israel. She had important positions in the Israeli government. In 1969 she was named Israel's fourth prime minister. She held that job until June 4, 1974.

FACTS

JOB

Photographer, environmentalist

BORN

February 20, 1902, U.S.A.

DIED

April 22, 1984

WHY HE'S IMPORTANT

His black-and-white nature photos helped make photography an art form.

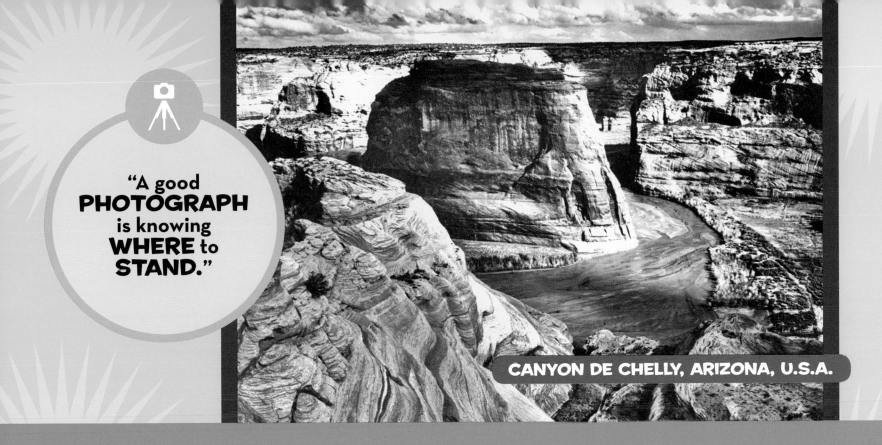

CANYON DE CHELLY, ARIZONA, U.S.A.

ANSEL ADAMS

When 14-year-old Ansel Adams visited Yosemite National Park in California, U.S.A., with his family, he used his Brownie box camera to take pictures. Adams spent many summers camping and hiking the Sierra Nevada mountain range. During every trip he used pictures as a way to remember where he'd been and what he'd seen.

Adams's **CROOKED NOSE** was caused by the San Francisco **EARTHQUAKE** of 1906. A powerful aftershock threw four-year-old Ansel **FACE** first into a **GARDEN WALL.**

Even though Adams gave up his dream of becoming a **CONCERT PIANIST,** he played the piano for **FUN** and **RELAXATION** for the rest of **HIS LIFE.**

Over the next few years, Adams bought better cameras and equipment. He read a lot of photography magazines. He attended photography exhibits. Even though Adams spent so much time studying photography, he never thought of his picture-taking as more than a hobby. What he really wanted to do was become a concert pianist.

Adams was well into his 20s and still trying to become a pianist and practice photography. There was so much to know about each. There were so many hours he needed to practice to become great. He finally realized that he had to choose one career or the other. He chose photography.

Before Ansel Adams came along, photographs weren't thought of as art. Ansel paid attention to how natural light and shadows highlighted his pictures. People then started seeing the beauty that photographs could capture. Adams also used his photos of the American West to urge people to protect the wilderness.

"Sometimes I do get to **PLACES** just when **GOD'S** ready to have somebody **CLICK** the **SHUTTER.**"

75

FACTS

JOB
Artist

BORN
July 6, 1907, Mexico

DIED
July 13, 1954

WHY SHE'S IMPORTANT
She is known for her bright, emotional paintings.

FRIDA KAHLO

Frida Kahlo wanted to be a doctor. But when she was 18, a bus she was riding in smashed into a streetcar. Kahlo was badly injured, and she could not go to medical school. She could not even walk and was stuck in bed for more than a year. To pass the time, she began painting. She used strong, bold colors that somehow *showed* her pain.

"SELF-PORTRAIT WITH MONKEY," FRIDA KAHLO, 1940

"I paint myself because I am so **OFTEN ALONE** and because I am the **SUBJECT** I know **BEST.**"

When Kahlo was 22 years old, she married a famous Mexican painter named Diego Rivera. Rivera told people that Kahlo was Mexico's best painter. Kahlo told people the same about Rivera.

Kahlo painted pictures of herself and her life struggles. Many people didn't like seeing paintings of somebody else's

Kahlo's many **PETS** included **SPIDER MONKEYS.**

DIEGO RIVERA AND FRIDA KAHLO, 1939

unhappiness. Kahlo kept painting anyway. Other painters have been inspired by her to do the same. Even when they have problems, they just keep on painting to help them express their feelings.

The Blue House in Mexico City where Kahlo grew up is now the Frida Kahlo Museum.

"I **PAINT FLOWERS** so they will **NOT** die."

FRIDA KAHLO MUSEUM, THE BLUE HOUSE, MEXICO CITY

FACTS

JOB

Mountaineer

BORN

May 29, 1914, Nepal

DIED

May 9, 1986

WHY HE'S IMPORTANT

He was a member of the first team to reach the summit (top) of Mount Everest.

At **29,029 FEET** (8,848 m) high, Mount Everest is the **TALLEST MOUNTAIN** on Earth.

TENZING NORGAY

Many dangers face those who want to climb to the top of Mount Everest. The air is thin at high altitudes, so it is hard for human lungs to get enough oxygen. Storms can move in quickly and bring high winds and very cold temperatures. Climbers often fall. Some might step into a deep gash in the ice called a crevasse. Dangerous avalanches can strike at any time. They sweep away everything and everybody in their path.

Tenzing Norgay grew up in the Himalayan mountains. He was a Sherpa. Men like him are hired by climbers. Sherpas do dangerous work such as breaking a trail through ice and snow, carrying supplies, and attaching climbing ropes to the mountain.

In the 1930s and 1940s, Sherpa Tenzing Norgay helped on many climbs up Mount Everest. Those groups had to turn back every time.

In 1953, Tenzing was helping a British group up the mountain. The first two climbers pushing for the summit (top) ran out of oxygen and had to turn back. Three days later, Tenzing and his climbing partner Edmund Hillary gave it a try.

TENZING HIKING IN NEPAL, 1953

SHERPAS are **HIMALAYAN** people from **NEPAL** or **TIBET** who are used to living and working in thin mountain air. They are **EXCELLENT** mountain **CLIMBERS**.

CHINA

Mount Everest

NEPAL

BHUTAN

INDIA

BANGLADESH

MYANMAR (BURMA)

Map Key
— Present-day country boundary

Bay of Bengal

Tenzing and Hillary reached the highest point on Earth on May 29, 1953. They were very excited. The two men shook hands and patted each other's backs. Back at camp they were asked which of them first set foot on the summit. Neither man would say.

Tenzing wrote a book about the climb that was published in 1955. Called *Tiger of the Snows,* the book revealed that Hillary was ahead of him.

"It has been a **LONG ROAD** ... From a ... bearer of loads, to a **WEARER OF A COAT** with rows of medals who is carried about in planes ..."

SIR EDMUND HILLARY AND TENZING NORGAY, ALL SMILES AFTER REACHING THE SUMMIT

FACTS

JOB
Singer

BORN
April 25, 1917, U.S.A.

DIED
June 15, 1996

WHY SHE'S IMPORTANT
She made popular a form of singing called scat. She was the first African-American woman to win a Grammy Award.

Fitzgerald could make her **VOICE** sound like a **TRUMPET**, a **SAXOPHONE**, or a **TROMBONE**.

"The **ONLY THING BETTER** than singing is more singing."

In **1934 teenager Ella Fitzgerald** stood just off-stage at Harlem's Apollo Theater in New York City. She was scared. Why? She'd won a chance to perform for Amateur Night. She'd planned to dance, but the act that went on right before her also danced. Those girls were *really* good. Fitzgerald made the last-minute decision to sing instead. That decision would change her life.

ELLA FITZGERALD

The audience loved Fitzgerald's singing. They jumped up and clapped wildly. Two months later, Fitzgerald started singing with a band led by a man named Chick Webb. She traveled with the band for a few years. When Webb died, she led the band herself for a while.

FITZGERALD WITH THE CHICK WEBB ORCHESTRA, 1936

In her long career, Ella Fitzgerald won **13 GRAMMY AWARDS** and sold over **40 MILLION ALBUMS.**

People couldn't seem to get enough of hearing Fitzgerald singing and swinging. She was given the nickname "the first lady of song." Before long, she became the most popular female jazz singer in the United States. Her amazing popularity lasted for 50 years. She won her first Grammy Award in 1958, followed by many more.

Ella Fitzgerald is most famous for making scat singing popular. In scat singing, a singer makes up the tune as she goes along. Instead of words, the singer uses lots of syllables like *shoo-be-boppa-hippa-dippa-doodah-doop-de-doop*. (Try it!)

"It isn't where **YOU CAME FROM**, it's where **YOU'RE GOING** that counts."

SINGING AND SWINGING, 1970

MEET MORE ARTISTS

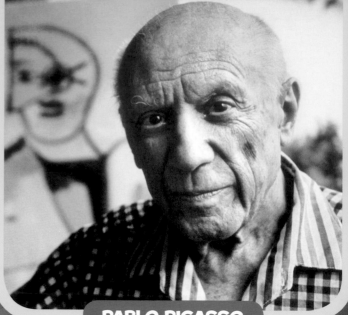

PABLO PICASSO

1887–1986, U.S.A. Georgia O'Keeffe loved painting flowers. When she was 42, she visited Santa Fe, New Mexico, U.S.A. The colors and shapes of the land and sky there inspired her. She began painting what she saw. For the next 40 years, O'Keeffe painted scenes of New Mexico. One of her most famous paintings is "Ram's Head."

GEORGIA O'KEEFFE

1881–1973, Spain. From the time he was a boy, Pablo Picasso's talent amazed older artists. He co-invented a type of painting called cubism, in which common things are painted in stretched-out shapes. Sometimes Picasso included a little dachshund in his paintings. This dog's name was Lump.

MAURICE SENDAK

WOLFGANG MOZART

1928–2012, U.S.A. Maurice Sendak wrote and illustrated children's books. His most famous book was *Where the Wild Things Are*. It won an award for the best illustrated American picture book of 1964. Sendak wrote and illustrated books his entire life. He also designed stage sets for plays.

1756–1791, Austria. Mozart was a musical genius. At 6 years old, he taught himself to play the piano. At 17, Mozart was composing operas and all kinds of classical music. In his 35 years, he wrote more than 600 pieces of music and influenced composers such as Ludwig van Beethoven and Joseph Haydn.

SHEL SILVERSTEIN

1930–1999, U.S.A. Shel Silverstein began drawing when he was seven years old. He grew up to become a cartoonist, a poet, a songwriter, and a storyteller. A picture book called *The Giving Tree* is his most popular work. He is also the author of the popular children's poetry books *Where the Sidewalk Ends* and *A Light in the Attic*. His poems are short, imaginative, and often very funny.

MIKHAIL BARYSHNIKOV

1948– , Russia. Mikhail Baryshnikov was one of the Soviet Union's most famous ballet dancers in the early 1970s. In 1974 he moved to the United States and soon joined the American Ballet Theater. He became famous in his new country. Today he works to promote ballet and is also an actor and choreographer.

LOUISA MAY ALCOTT

1832–1888, U.S.A. Louisa May Alcott published stories, poems, and plays using a pseudonym (made-up name) because women were discouraged from becoming writers in her time. She finally started using her real name when she began writing books. The book that made her famous was *Little Women*. It is still popular today.

BERTHE MORISOT

1841–1895, France. Berthe Morisot loved painting at a time when people thought women should not be artists. Morisot became famous for her Impressionist paintings. This style of painting uses bold brush strokes, rich colors, and sunlight to show everyday moments in a way that makes people feel emotional.

JACKIE ROBINSON

Jackie Robinson was the first athlete at the University of California, Los Angeles (UCLA), to win varsity letters in four sports: baseball, basketball, football, and track. When he was 23, Robinson joined the U.S. Army. After his time in the Army, Robinson played a season of professional baseball for the Kansas City (U.S.A.) Monarchs. They were a team in the Negro Leagues. The Negro Leagues were baseball leagues made up of African-American players.

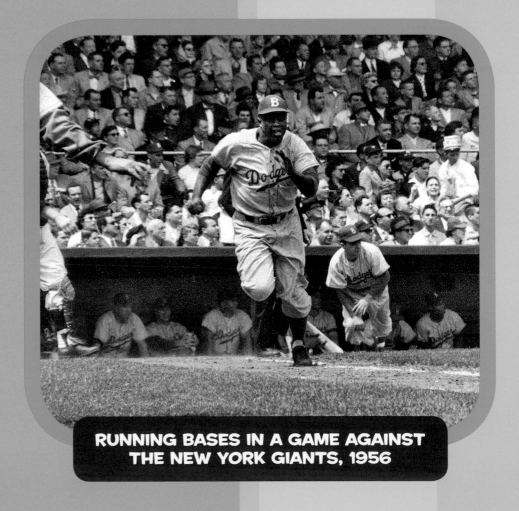

RUNNING BASES IN A GAME AGAINST THE NEW YORK GIANTS, 1956

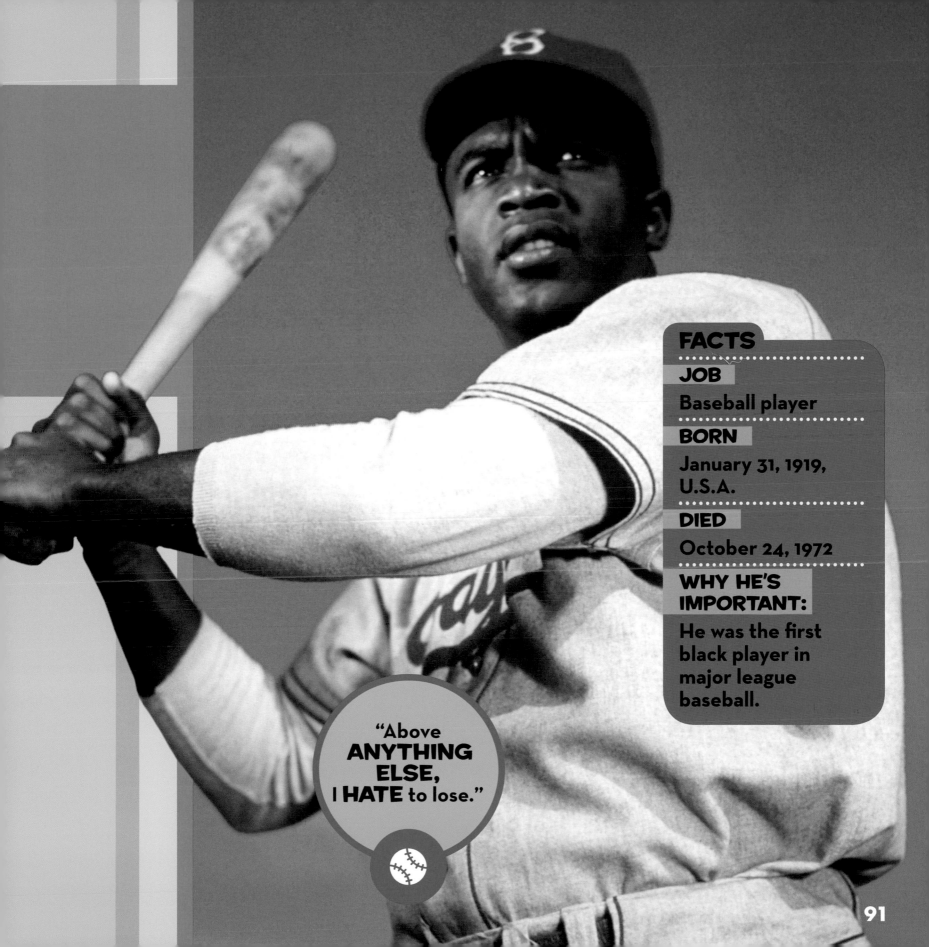

FACTS

JOB
Baseball player

BORN
January 31, 1919, U.S.A.

DIED
October 24, 1972

WHY HE'S IMPORTANT:
He was the first black player in major league baseball.

"Above **ANYTHING ELSE,** I **HATE** to lose."

"How you **PLAYED** in yesterday's game is **ALL THAT COUNTS.**"

In 1946 Brooklyn Dodgers manager Branch Rickey asked Robinson to play for his team. No major league baseball team had ever had a black player. Robinson was an excellent athlete, and Rickey hoped he would do so well that fans and other players might like having him be part of the Dodgers team. Rickey warned Robinson that some people would be upset to see a black player in the white leagues. He told Robinson that they might yell mean things at him. But it would be important that Robinson not lose his temper.

ROBINSON PLAYED FOR MONTREAL IN A 1947 EXHIBITION GAME AGAINST HIS FUTURE TEAM, THE DODGERS.

When Robinson was a **YOUNG MAN,** professional sports teams were **SEGREGATED.** There were teams with either all **WHITE MEN** or all **BLACK MEN AS PLAYERS. THOSE** teams only played against teams that looked like them.

Jackie Robinson was **VOTED** into the **BASEBALL HALL OF FAME** in 1962.

ROOKIE OF THE YEAR
19 47
JACKIE ROBINSON

I'M ROOTING FOR JACKIE ROBINSON
DODGERS

A Fawcett Publication

Jackie Robinson

10¢

Special!
INSIDE THE DODGER TRAINING CAMP!
READ
ROOKIE ON TRIAL!

JACKIE ROBINSON COMIC BOOK, 1951

Some fans shouted awful things at Robinson every time he was up to bat. He chose not to respond to it, and just played his hardest. By the end of the season, his play had shown fans he was a great baseball player. In that first year, he hit 12 home runs, led the league in stolen bases (29), and was named Rookie of the Year.

With the Dodgers, Jackie Robinson played first base, second base, third base, and left field. He stole bases 197 times, and even stole home 11 times!

93

MAYA ANGELOU

Maya Angelou was named Marguerite Annie Johnson when she was born. At age seven, her parents broke up, and she was sent to live with her grandmother. The rest of her childhood was so rough that she stopped talking for a long time.

ANGELOU WITH HER BOOK, *I KNOW WHY THE CAGED BIRD SINGS, 1971*

FACTS

JOB

Poet, writer, actress, dancer, singer

BORN

April 4, 1928, U.S.A.

DIED

May 28, 2014

WHY SHE'S IMPORTANT

Her book of poems was the first collection written by an African-American woman to become a best seller.

"A bird **DOESN'T SING** because it has an **ANSWER**, it sings because it has a **SONG.**"

By the time she was a teenager, Marguerite knew she wanted to be an entertainer. She moved to California to live with her mother and to study dance and acting. In her mid-20s, Marguerite's career was taking off. She was working as a singer when she changed her name to Maya Angelou. Angelou appeared in many stage plays and even released a music album called *Miss Calypso*. She was also a writer and worked for civil rights alongside Martin Luther King, Jr.

A SCENE FROM THE 1995 MOVIE *HOW TO MAKE AN AMERICAN QUILT*

"People **WILL FORGET** what you **SAID**, people will forget what you **DID**, but people will never forget how you **MADE THEM FEEL.**"

Angelou wanted to do many things. She was always ready to try something new. A friend suggested that she write a book about her difficult childhood, and she did. She called it *I Know Why the Caged Bird Sings*. The book won many awards and made her famous around the world.

In 1993 Maya Angelou **READ ALOUD** one of her **POEMS**, "On the Pulse of Morning," at President Bill **CLINTON'S INAUGURATION.**

SOME OF ANGELOU'S BOOKS ON DISPLAY

THE COLLECTED AUTOBIOGRAPHIES of MAYA ANGELOU

Maya Angelou went on to write more books and songs, act, and even direct a movie. Over the years she won many awards for her work in entertainment and civil rights. Even though she did many important things, people are most inspired by her strong, wise words.

MARTIN LUTHER KING, JR.

When Martin Luther King, Jr., was growing up in Georgia, African-American children went to different schools from white children. That was the law across all southern U.S. states.

Keeping **RACES APART,** treating one as though it is **LESS IMPORTANT,** is called **SEGREGATION.**

FACTS

JOB

Baptist minister

BORN

January 15, 1929,
U.S.A.

DIED

April 4, 1968

WHY HE'S IMPORTANT

He used peaceful protests and demonstrations to call for equality between black and white Americans. He was an important leader in the civil rights movement in the United States.

When African Americans left their homes to go to restaurants, movie theaters, or anywhere, they had to stand, sit—even drink water and go to the bathroom—in places separate from whites. In most parts of the South, they were not allowed to vote. If they didn't obey the rules, they risked violence from whites or were even arrested.

Martin Luther King, Jr., knew segregation was wrong. He knew that all people should be treated equally, with kindness and respect, no matter what color skin they have.

"**LOVE** is the only force capable of **TRANSFORMING** an **ENEMY** into a **FRIEND.**"

KING WAVES TO THE CROWD AFTER HIS 1963 "I HAVE A DREAM" SPEECH IN WASHINGTON, D.C.

King worked to end segregation and gain equal rights. He also worked to help others understand why inequality was wrong. He led marches, wrote books and magazine articles, and talked to newspaper reporters and anyone else who would listen. Just like Gandhi, King believed that there were peaceful ways to change society for the better. He knew violence was not the answer.

After an African-American woman named **ROSA PARKS** was arrested for refusing to **GIVE UP** her **BUS SEAT** to a white man, King **LED** the fight to get the law changed.

DR. MARTIN LUTHER KING, JR. MEMORIAL, WASHINGTON, D.C.

Congress passed the Civil Rights Act in 1964. Just four years later, King was assassinated—killed by a racist person who didn't like him or agree with his cause. The Civil Rights Act ended segregation and made it illegal to treat people differently because of their race or nationality, religion, or whether they were men or women.

FACTS

JOB

Astronaut

BORN

August 5, 1930, U.S.A.

DIED

August 25, 2012

WHY HE'S IMPORTANT

He was the first person to walk on the moon.

NEIL ARMSTRONG

When engineer Neil Armstrong joined the organization that would soon become known as NASA (National Aeronautics and Space Administration), he knew his favorite part of the job would be working as a test pilot.

Armstrong flew **DOZENS OF GLIDERS,** helicopters, jets, and rockets. He tested the rocket-powered X-15, which could fly (6,437 km/h) **4,000 MILES AN HOUR!**

ARMSTRONG PRACTICING FOR APOLLO 11 MISSION, 1969

Armstrong started astronaut training in 1962. In 1966 he was chosen as command pilot for his first mission, called Gemini VIII. During that flight, Armstrong became the first person to successfully join together two space vehicles.

Apollo 11 was the spaceflight that put the first humans on the moon. Armstrong was the spacecraft commander. On July 16, 1969, Armstrong stepped onto the moon's dusty surface. He was just ahead of fellow astronaut Edwin E. "Buzz" Aldrin. The third astronaut, Michael Collins, stayed on the ship. While on the moon, Armstrong had a message for listeners at NASA and the millions watching on TV around the world: "That's one small step for man, one giant leap for mankind."

Armstrong and Aldrin **SEPARATED** from their main spacecraft **TO LAND ON THE MOON** in a module named *EAGLE.*

"Gliders, sail planes, they're **WONDERFUL FLYING MACHINES.** It's the closest you can come to being a **BIRD.**"

ARMSTRONG ON THE MOON, 1969

Armstrong and Aldrin bounced around on the moon's dusty surface for two and a half hours. They conducted experiments and collected rocks and soil samples.

When they returned to Earth, the three astronauts were treated like heroes. They were given medals and celebrated at parades.

Armstrong became very famous, but he preferred to live a quiet life. He taught college students until 1979. When he retired he bought a farm in Ohio and raised cattle and corn.

ARMSTRONG IN AN EARLY SPACE SUIT

"I **AM**, and **EVER WILL BE,** a white socks, pocket protector, **NERDY** engineer."

PARADE HONORING APOLLO ASTRONAUTS, NEW YORK CITY

DONG ZHIMING

Dong Zhiming was 13 years old when he saw his first dinosaur exhibit. He still remembers standing in front of a huge, five-foot (1.5-m)-long leg bone that had belonged to a hadrosaur (a duck-billed plant-eater). That's the day he got hooked on dinosaurs.

GIANT DUCK-BILLED DINOSAUR SKELETON

Dong Zhiming **FOUND** a **DINOSAUR** at a gas and oil company's **CONSTRUCTION SITE.** He named that dinosaur *GASOSAURUS CONSTRUCTUS.*

FACTS

JOB
Paleontologist

BORN
January 1937, China

WHY HE'S IMPORTANT
He is one of the most successful dinosaur fossil hunters in the world.

He lived in China. It was a good place for dinosaur hunting. China is rich in fossils. Many can be found in the northwestern river valleys and parts of the Gobi desert. After studying dinosaurs in college, Dong got a job working with other dinosaur hunters in the city of Beijing.

His first trip out with the group was to a place where dinosaur bones had been found before. After hours of searching, he saw a small, rounded shape poking out of the sunbaked dirt. It was part of the backbone of an enormous sauropod (a long-necked dinosaur like *Apatosaurus*).

DONG GETS A LIFT TO STUDY THE NECK OF AN OMEISAUR.

Dong's most exciting find was on a hilltop in southwest China. The hill was being flattened for a parking lot. Moving all that dirt had revealed dinosaur bones. Lots of dinosaur bones. "We've found a dinosaur graveyard!" Dong shouted to his friends. All the bones were from the middle Jurassic period (about 160 million years ago). The site became known as the Dashanpu Formation. It is now the home of one of the best dinosaur museums in the world.

"It remains a **MYSTERY** as to what caused the species to **DISAPPEAR** from the face of **THE EARTH** ... it's my intention to devote my **ENTIRE LIFE** towards unraveling the **MYSTERY.**"

Dong found so many fossils over the years that he lost count of how many he discovered. Many of them were from dinosaurs never seen before. He named more than 20 dinosaurs. Sometimes they were named after the places where they were found. Sometimes he named them after friends.

GOBI DESERT

● Beijing

CHINA

★ Dashanpu Formation

Map Key
— Country boundary

FACTS

JOB
Musicians

BORN
Early 1940s,
England

DIED
John Lennon, 1980.
George Harrison,
2001.

**WHY THEY'RE
IMPORTANT**
They were one of
the most influential
rock-and-roll bands
in history.

THE BEATLES

In January 1962 four young men from Liverpool, England, traveled to London to play some songs for a record company. They hoped the company would record their music and introduce them to the world. But the company said no. The Beatles were told that nobody wanted to hear guitar groups anymore.

Those four young men, the Beatles, went on to become the most famous rock band in the world. But it didn't happen overnight. They started out playing for small crowds in cities like Liverpool, England, and Hamburg, Germany. They didn't make much money, but people liked their music. Slowly, they became popular.

♪ "Count your **AGE** by **FRIENDS**, not years. Count your **LIFE** by **SMILES**, not tears." —John **LENNON**

♪ The Beatles included Ringo **STARR**, George **HARRISON**, Paul **MCCARTNEY**, and John **LENNON**.

PHOTO USED ON THEIR *TWIST AND SHOUT* ALBUM

On December 26, 1963, a song called "I Want to Hold Your Hand" was released in the United States. Fans bought 250,000 copies in the first three days! Americans loved this band! Radio stations played their songs over and over again.

PERFORMING ON A BRITISH TV SHOW CALLED *TOP OF THE POPS*, 1964

♫

"If I want to **SAY ANYTHING,** I write a **SONG.**" —Paul **MCCARTNEY**

On February 7, 1964, the band arrived in New York City. Excited fans packed every corner of the airport. The Beatles spent ten days in America, and fans followed them everywhere they went. On a Sunday evening in February 1964, the Beatles performed live on a program called *The Ed Sullivan Show*. Almost half of the televisions in American homes were tuned in to watch. Rock-and-roll was never the same.

THE BEATLES

♪ The **WEEK** of April 4, **1964**, the Beatles had the **TOP FIVE** most **POPULAR** songs in the United States.

PHOTO USED ON THE *ABBEY ROAD* ALBUM

FACTS

JOB

President of Chile

BORN

September 29, 1951, Chile

WHY SHE'S IMPORTANT

She worked to bring democracy to Chile, and she is the country's first female president. She also led the first United Nations agency devoted to women.

MICHELLE BACHELET

When Michelle Bachelet was a college student, she was pulled away from her studies and exiled (sent away) from Chile because the country's dictator didn't like her family's ideas on how things should be done there.

A **DICTATOR** uses **FORCE** to become the **HEAD OF A COUNTRY.** A dictator doesn't listen to the people and uses **SOLDIERS** to make them follow the rules.

PRESIDENT BACHELET GETS A SALUTE FROM THE PALACE GUARD BEFORE TAKING OFFICE.

SUPPORTERS OF PRESIDENT BACHELET, 2006

"I KNOW from my own experience that there is NO LIMIT TO WHAT WOMEN CAN DO."

Bachelet returned to Chile after a few years and completed medical school. She was still upset that Chile was being run by a dictator. She decided to join others who wanted democracy for their country. That finally happened in October 1988. Bachelet later worked for the new, democratic Chile as the minister of health. She later studied military strategy in the United States and then became Chile's minister of national defense.

PACIFIC OCEAN

SOUTH AMERICA

CHILE

ATLANTIC OCEAN

Map Key
— Country boundary

PRESIDENT BACHELET SPEAKS TO THE CHILEAN PEOPLE.

Bachelet almost said no when she was asked to run for president. But by then she was well known and popular in Chile. She was elected president not once but twice. Her first term was from 2006 to 2010. Her second one began in 2014.

From 2010 to 2014 Bachelet served as the first executive director of a United Nations organization called UN Women. The group is made up of leaders from around the world. Its goal is to make sure women everywhere are treated the same as men.

CHILEAN PRESIDENT MICHELLE BACHELET AND U.S. PRESIDENT BARACK OBAMA

MALALA YOUSAFZAI

When the Taliban began attacking girls' schools in the area of Pakistan where Malala Yousafzai lived, she gave a speech about it in her region's capital city, Peshawar.

Her talk was titled "How Dare the Taliban Take Away My Basic Right to Education?" That was in 2008. Malala was only ten years old.

JOB

Activist

BORN

July 12, 1997, Pakistan

WHY SHE'S IMPORTANT

She speaks out for the education of girls in her country, even after being shot for it.

The **TALIBAN** are a group of Afghan fighters who use **VIOLENCE** to **GET WHAT THEY WANT.**

Malala was 11 years old when she started writing a blog for the British Broadcasting Corporation (BBC). She wrote about living under threats from the Taliban. They don't believe girls should go to school. She was asked to use a fake name to protect herself, but her identity was impossible to hide forever.

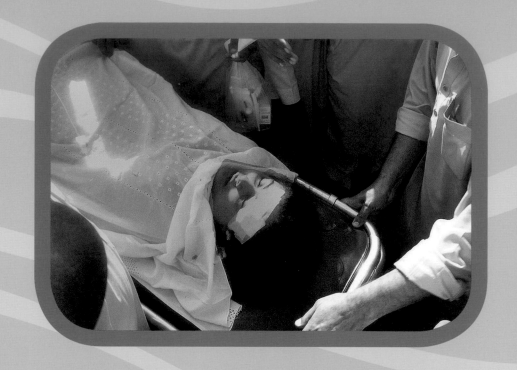

Malala was on her way home from school one day when a Taliban gunman entered her bus. He shot her in the head. Malala clung to life. She was flown to a military hospital in Peshawar, then moved to a hospital in England.

Malala Yousafzai plans to **BECOME A LAWYER** and return to **PAKISTAN.**

YOUSAFZAI SUPPORTERS PROTEST AGAINST THOSE WHO TRIED TO HARM HER.

Malala slowly healed. In March 2013 she was able to begin school in England. People around the world sent their support for the brave 14-year-old girl who had stood up to the Taliban.

Malala wrote a book about her experiences. She also continues to speak out for the rights of women and children in her country to get an education. She even gave a speech at the United Nations.

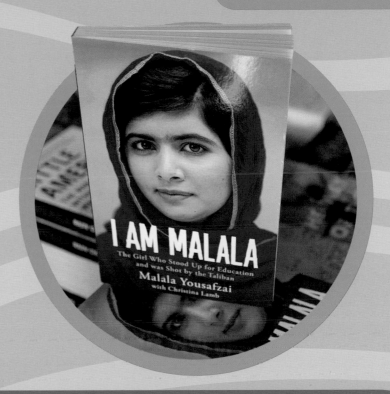

YOUSAFZAI SIGNS A GUEST BOOK AT THE UNITED NATIONS, NEW YORK CITY, IN 2013.

In 2014 Malala Yousafzai became the **YOUNGEST PERSON** in history to win a **NOBEL PEACE PRIZE.**

MEET MORE
HUMAN RIGHTS
LEADERS

THURGOOD MARSHALL

1908–1993, U.S.A. In 1954 lawyer Thurgood Marshall won an important case, *Brown* v. *Board of Education*. This case started in Topeka, Kansas, and went all the way to the U.S. Supreme Court. The Supreme Court decision made it against the law for U.S. public schools to separate students by race. Marshall continued working for equality and civil rights. In 1967 he became the first African American to be named a Supreme Court justice.

ELEANOR ROOSEVELT

1884–1962, U.S.A. Eleanor Roosevelt was the wife of President Franklin Roosevelt. President Roosevelt suffered from a disease called polio. It left him unable to stand, so Eleanor often gave speeches for him. She was involved in many political and human rights causes. She even represented the United States at the United Nations, where she spoke out for human rights.

HELEN KELLER

1880–1968, U.S.A. When Helen Keller was little, an illness left her blind and deaf. When she was seven, a teacher named Annie Sullivan taught her how to spell with her fingers. This changed her life. Keller grew up to become the first blind and deaf person to graduate from college. She then spent the rest of her life encouraging others with disabilities.

CESAR CHAVEZ

1927–1993, U.S.A. Cesar Chavez was very poor as a boy and had to work on many different farms. Workers were given low pay, poor housing, and little or no health care. Chavez wanted to change this. He co-founded a union called the National Farm Workers Association. Chavez spent the rest of his life trying to improve conditions for farm workers.

NELSON MANDELA

1918-2013, **South Africa.** Nelson Mandela spent 27 years in prison for leading South Africans in peaceful protests against apartheid (the South African word for making people live, eat, worship, and go to school only with other people who have the same skin color). In prison, Mandela studied to become a lawyer. A few years before apartheid ended, he was freed. In 1994 Mandela became his country's first black president.

WANGARI MAATHAI

1940-2011, **Kenya.** Wangari Maathai attended college in the United States. When she returned to her home in Kenya, she was shocked at what she saw. Environmental problems had turned the beautiful green countryside she loved into a dry, sunbaked wasteland. Most trees had been cut down for firewood, and there was little water. Maathai decided she wanted to do something to protect this land. She created the Green Belt Movement to teach women to plant and tend trees to help keep the land healthy.

HARRIET TUBMAN

1820-1913, **U.S.A.** Harriet Tubman escaped from slavery in 1848. She had her freedom but wanted to help other Maryland slaves escape. She did that again and again, using a secret route nicknamed the Underground Railroad. Tubman returned to plantations in Maryland to rescue other slaves. During the Civil War, she worked for the Union Army as a cook, nurse, and spy.

THE 14TH DALAI LAMA, TENZIN GYATSO

1935- , **China.** The religious leader of Buddhism in Tibet is known as the Dalai Lama. Tenzin Gyatso became the 14th Dalai Lama when he was 15. He travels the world, teaching others that a happy life is found through compassion (concern and sympathy for others). He urges listeners to care for the environment, treat all people equally, and seek peace.

PARENT TIPS

Extend your child's experience beyond the pages of this book. Visits to historical sites and museums are a great way to continue satisfying your child's curiosity about people from all over the world. Encourage your little one to talk about the people he or she admires most, real or imaginary, and discuss why those people are so important. Here are some other activities you can do with National Geographic's *Little Kids First Big Book of Who*.

LITTLE ARTIST
(ARTS AND CRAFTS)

Create a masterpiece with your little one. Gather markers, colored pencils, paint, or crayons in a variety of colors, and make sure you have plenty of white paper to work on. Before starting, present your child with examples of colorful artwork from artists like Pablo Picasso and Georgia O'Keeffe. As your little artist begins to choose colors, ask her how different colors or shapes make her feel. Once your child is finished, hang the piece of art where it can be seen and compare it to the examples of colorful artwork you viewed before starting.

AROUND THE WORLD
(GEOGRAPHY)

Amelia Earhart was the first female to fly solo across the Atlantic Ocean. She began her journey in Harbour Grace, Newfoundland, and ended it on the other side of the ocean in Derry, Northern Ireland. Look at a map with your child to track Earhart's long trip. Point out Northern Ireland's surrounding areas, such as France, where she originally intended to land her plane, and discuss where you live in relation to the voyage.

THE PEOPLE IN YOUR POCKET
(MATH)

Money is everywhere and many banknotes and coins from different countries feature images of the people who have made a difference there. Working with coins, teach your child how to count. Separate the different coins you have and discuss the famous faces that might appear on each of them. Who are they? Why are they important? You and your little one can start by counting how many coins there are in each group before graduating to counting how much each group is worth.

PLAY BALL
(HAND-EYE COORDINATION)

Teach your child how to play catch like the famous baseball player Jackie Robinson. Start by sitting straddled a few feet from each other on the ground. Roll a light rubber ball back and forth, aiming for the belly button. The ball should be an appropriate size for the age of the child participating in this game. If you hit your target, you earn a point. Once rolling the ball becomes more comfortable, advance to tossing the ball to each other while standing up. Encourage your child to follow the ball with his eyes until he is able to catch it in both of his hands.

SING LIKE ELLA
(MUSIC)

Introduce your little one to Ella Fitzgerald and Louis Armstrong's "Dream a Little Dream of Me." If you don't already know it, the tune can be found online. Together, listen carefully for Ella's special scat singing, in which she sings the tune in syllables instead of words. Once you've heard her example, encourage your child to try the same type of singing. You can use "Dream a Little Dream of Me" or you can try scat singing to your child's favorite songs. Talk with your child about how the music sounds and how it makes her feel.

WATCH BACK-YARD WILDLIFE (OBSERVATION)

Study wildlife just as Jane Goodall did. Accompany your little one outside with a notebook and a pencil. Together, search for an animal and watch it closely from afar. Have your child talk about what he sees—an insect's actions, what it likes to eat, and how it moves in its environment, for example. Ask him to write down the observations and then read them aloud once you're finished watching the creature. Work together to draw a picture of what you observed.

ONCE UPON A TIME (STORYTELLING)

Practice writing stories like the famous authors in this book. Ask your child to tell you an exciting adventure story using her imagination. Write down the details of the story as you're listening or record it. Once she is finished, read the story out loud and work together on illustrations that will help the story come to life. Have her create a cover and write a title for her book.

ACT IT OUT (COMMUNICATION)

Try communicating with your kids without speaking, as Helen Keller did. Cut up small pieces of paper and write out different words, actions, and places on each. Fold the pieces of paper and shuffle them all together. Take turns acting out a word from the pile while trying to get the other players to guess what it is. You can move your body and make sounds, but you can't use any words! Discuss the difficulties of trying to communicate without being able to speak.

MATCHING GAME (POETRY AND MATCHING)

Read a favorite rhyming poem to your child. Together, pick out the words that rhyme with one another and help your little one write each of them on individual index cards. Shuffle the cards so the rhyming words are no longer together and spread them face up so that all of the words can be seen. Then, work with your child to pair the rhyming words together again.

FURTHER READING

KING TUT: Zoehfeld, Kathleen Weidner, and James Nelson. *The Curse of King Tut's Mummy*. Random House Books for Young Readers, 2007.

SHAKESPEARE: Stanley, Diane, and Peter Vennema. *Bard of Avon: The Story of William Shakespeare*. HarperCollins, 1998.

SEQUOYAH: Rumford, James. *Sequoyah: The Cherokee Man Who Gave His People Writing*. HMH Books for Young Readers, 2004.

SACAGAWEA: Buffalohead, Julie, and Liselotte Erdich. *Sacagawea*. Carolrhoda Books, 2003.

LINCOLN: Gilpin, Caroline Crosson. *National Geographic Readers: Abraham Lincoln*. National Geographic Society, 2012.

BLACKWELL: Stone, Tanya Lee. *Who Says Women Can't Be Doctors?: The Story of Elizabeth Blackwell*. Henry Holt & Co., 2013.

HENSON: Hopkinson, Deborah, and Stephen Alcorn. *Keep On!: The Story of Matthew Henson, Co-Discoverer of the North Pole*. Peachtree Publishers, 2009.

CURIE: MacLeod, Elizabeth, and John Mantha. *Marie Curie*. Kids Can Press, 2009.

EARHART: Gilpin, Caroline. *National Geographic Readers: Amelia Earhart*. National Geographic Society, 2013.

MEIR: Krasner, Barbara, and Kelsey Garrity-Riley. *Goldie Takes a Stand: Golda Meir's First Crusade*. Kar-Ben Publishing, 2014.

KAHLO: Frith, Margaret, and Tomie dePaola. *Frida Kahlo: The Artist Who Painted Herself*. Grosset & Dunlap, 2003.

FITZGERALD: Pinkney, Andrea Davis, and Brian Pinkney. *Ella Fitzgerald: The Tale of a Vocal Virtuosa*. Jump at the Sun, 2007.

ROBINSON: Meltzer, Brad, and Christopher Eliopoulos. *I Am Jackie Robinson*. Dial Books for Young Readers, 2015.

KING: Rappaport, Doreen, and Bryan Collier. *Martin's Big Words: The Life of Dr. Martin Luther King, Jr.* Hyperion Books, 2007.

YOUSAFZAI: Abouraya, Karen Leggett, and L.C. Wheatley. *Malala Yousafzai: Warrior With Words*. StarWalk Kids Media, 2014.

GLOSSARY

ACTIVIST: someone who works for social change to help make life better for others

ALTITUDE: how high something is above the level of the sea

AMATEUR NIGHT: a type of show that takes place at night in which a person can participate to show his or her talent

ANCIENT: very, very old

CHOREOGRAPHER (DANCE): a person who creates steps and moves for dancers

CIVIL RIGHTS: the rights of people to be treated equally and without discrimination; rights that protect each person's personal and legal freedoms

COFFIN: the box in which a dead body is buried

COMPOSE (MUSIC): create and arrange the musical notes that make up a song

DEMOCRACY: a type of government in which everybody is allowed to vote and have their say about the way things are done in political life

DETERMINED: when one's mind is made up and he or she is set on following that path

ELECT: vote someone into a position (job)

ENROLL: enter a school officially; sign up

EXHIBIT: display for others to see, as in an art gallery or museum

EXPEDITION: journey or trip taken by a group for some reason, as in climbing a mountain or exploring a new place

FOSSIL: the imprint of a prehistoric organism in another material (for example, a leaf imprint in a rock) or a bone that has petrified (turned to stone)

GENIUS: a very creative or intelligent person

HUMAN RIGHTS: rights that belong to every person. Freedom is an example of a human right.

INDEPENDENT: free from anybody else's control; not connected with anything else

INTERPRETER: a person who helps two people who speak different languages understand one another

MUMMY: an ancient body that has been preserved and wrapped in cloth

NAVIGATE: find a way from one place to another

NOVELIST: a person who writes novels (fiction, or made-up, stories)

PALEONTOLOGY: study of fossilized animals and plants

PROTEST: public show of disapproval

PUBLISHER: a company that makes books and magazines

RADIOACTIVE: giving off dangerous, invisible waves or particles

REGION: area

REPRESENT: speak and act for others

SCAFFOLDING: temporary structure that helps workers reach high places

SOUTHERN HEMISPHERE: the half of Earth that is south of the Equator

SYLLABARY: written characters that represent sounds

UNDERGROUND RAILROAD: a secret path used by slaves in the southern United States to escape to free states in the North and to Canada.

UNITED NATIONS: an organization made up of representatives from countries around the world whose purpose is to promote peace and cooperation

URGE: try to make a person do something; strongly encourage

VIOLENCE: fighting that is meant to hurt another person

INDEX

Boldface indicates illustrations.